Martin Luther King Jr.

The Biography

GW00455854

0

Introduction

Martin Luther King Jr. was a Baptist minister and civil-rights activist who had a seismic impact on race relations in the United States, beginning in the mid-1950s.

Among his many efforts, King headed the Southern Christian Leadership Conference (SCLC). Through his activism and inspirational speeches, he played a pivotal role in ending the legal segregation of African American citizens in the United States, as well as the creation of the Civil Rights Act of 1964 and the Voting Rights Act of 1965.

King won the Nobel Peace Prize in 1964, among several other honors. He continues to be remembered as one of the most influential and inspirational African American leaders in history.

"The time is always right to do what is right." — Martin Luther King Jr

This is the descriptive, concise biography of Martin Luther King Jr.

Table of Contents

Martin Luther King Jr

Martin Luther King Jr. (born Michael King Jr.; January 15, 1929 – April 4, 1968) was an African American Baptist minister and activist who became the most visible spokesperson and leader in the American civil rights movement from 1955 until his assassination in 1968. King advanced civil rights through nonviolence and civil disobedience, inspired by his Christian beliefs and the nonviolent activism of Mahatma Gandhi. He was the son of early civil rights activist Martin Luther King Sr.

King participated in and led marches for blacks' right to vote, desegregation, labor rights, and other basic civil rights. King led the 1955 Montgomery bus boycott and later became the first president of the Southern Christian Leadership Conference (SCLC). As president of the SCLC, he led the unsuccessful Albany Movement in Albany, Georgia, and helped organize some of the nonviolent 1963 protests in Birmingham, Alabama. King helped organize the 1963 March on Washington, where he delivered his famous "I Have a Dream" speech on the steps of the Lincoln Memorial.

The SCLC put into practice the tactics of nonviolent protest with some success by strategically choosing the methods and places in which protests were carried out. There were several dramatic stand-offs with segregationist authorities, who sometimes turned violent. FBI Director J. Edgar Hoover considered King a radical and made him an object of the FBI's COINTELPRO from 1963, forward. FBI agents investigated him for possible communist ties, recorded his extramarital affairs and reported on them to government officials, and, in 1964, mailed King a threatening anonymous letter, which he interpreted as an attempt to make him commit suicide.

On October 14, 1964, King won the Nobel Peace Prize for combating racial inequality through nonviolent resistance. In 1965, he helped organize two of the three Selma to Montgomery marches. In his final years, he expanded his focus to include opposition towards poverty, capitalism, and the Vietnam War.

In 1968, King was planning a national occupation of Washington, D.C., to be called the Poor People's Campaign, when he was assassinated on April 4 in Memphis, Tennessee. His death was followed by riots in many U.S. cities. Allegations that James Earl Ray, the man convicted of killing King, had been framed or acted in concert with government agents persisted for decades after the shooting. King was posthumously awarded the Presidential Medal of Freedom in 1977 and the Congressional Gold Medal in 2003.

Martin Luther King Jr. Day was established as a holiday in cities and states throughout the United States beginning in 1971; the holiday was enacted at the federal level by legislation signed by President Ronald Reagan in 1986.

Hundreds of streets in the U.S. have been renamed in his honor, and the most populous county in Washington State was rededicated for him. The Martin Luther King Jr. Memorial on the National Mall in Washington, D.C., was dedicated in 2011.

Fact: King is the only non-president to have a national holiday in his name: The holiday, first commemorated in 1986, is celebrated on the third Monday in January, close to the civil rights leader's January 15 birthday.

Early life and education

Birth

King was born Michael King Jr. on January 15, 1929, in Atlanta, Georgia, the second of three children to the Reverend Michael King and Alberta King (née Williams). King's mother named him Michael, which was entered onto the birth certificate by the attending physician.

King's older sister is Christine King Farris and his younger brother was Alfred Daniel "A.D." King. King's maternal grandfather Adam Daniel Williams, who was a minister in rural Georgia, moved to Atlanta in 1893, and became pastor of the Ebenezer Baptist Church in the following year. Williams was of African-Irish descent. Williams married Jennie Celeste Parks, who gave birth to King's mother, Alberta. King's father was born to sharecroppers, James Albert and Delia King of Stockbridge, Georgia.

In his adolescent years, King Sr. left his parents' farm and walked to Atlanta where he attained a high school education. King Sr. then enrolled in Morehouse College and studied to enter the ministry. King Sr. and Alberta began dating in 1920, and married on November 25, 1926. Until Jennie's death in 1941, they lived together on the second floor of her parent's two-story Victorian house, where King was born.

Shortly after marrying Alberta, King Sr. became assistant pastor of the Ebenezer Baptist Church. Adam Daniel Williams died of a stroke in the spring of 1931. That fall,

King's father took over the role of pastor at the church, where he would in time raise the attendance from six hundred to several thousand.

In 1934, the church sent King Sr. on a multinational trip to Rome, Tunisia, Egypt, Jerusalem, Bethlehem, then Berlin for the meeting of the Baptist World Alliance (BWA). The trip ended with visits to sites in Berlin associated with the Reformation leader, Martin Luther. While there, Michael King Sr. witnessed the rise of Nazism. In reaction, the BWA conference issued a resolution which stated, "This Congress deplores and condemns as a violation of the law of God the Heavenly Father, all racial animosity, and every form of oppression or unfair discrimination toward the Jews, toward coloured people, or toward subject races in any part of the world."

He returned home in August 1934, and in that same year began referring to himself as Martin Luther King, and his son as Martin Luther King Jr. King's birth certificate was altered to read "Martin Luther King Jr." on July 23, 1957, when he was 28 years old.

Early childhood

"I have a dream that my four little children will one day live in a nation where they will not be judged by the color of their skin but by the content of their character."
— Martin Luther King Jr

At his childhood home, King and his two siblings would read aloud the Bible as instructed by their father. After dinners there, King's grandmother Jennie, who he affectionately referred to as "Mama", would tell lively stories from the Bible to her grandchildren. King's father would regularly use whippings to discipline his children.

At times, King Sr. would also have his children whip each other. King's father later remarked, "[King] was the most peculiar child whenever you whipped him. He'd stand there, and the tears would run down, and he'd never cry." Once when King witnessed his brother A.D. emotionally upset his sister Christine, he took a telephone and knocked out A.D. with it. When he and his brother were playing at their home, A.D. slid from a banister and hit into their grandmother, Jennie, causing her to fall down unresponsive. King, believing her dead, blamed himself and attempted suicide by jumping from a second-story window. Upon hearing that his grandmother was alive, King rose and left the ground where he had fallen.

King became friends with a white boy whose father owned a business across the street from his family's home. In September 1935, when the boys were about six years old, they started school. King had to attend a school for black children, Younge Street Elementary School, while his close playmate went to a separate school for white children only. Soon afterwards, the parents of the white boy stopped allowing King to play with their son, stating to him "we are white, and you are colored". When King relayed the happenings to his parents, they had a long discussion with him about the history of slavery and racism in America.

Upon learning of the hatred, violence and oppression that black people had faced in the U.S., King would later state that he was "determined to hate every white person". His parents instructed him that it was his Christian duty to love everyone.

King witnessed his father stand up against segregation and various forms of discrimination. Once, when stopped by a police officer who referred to King Sr. as "boy", King's father responded sharply that King was a boy but he was a man. When King's father took him into a shoe store in downtown Atlanta, the clerk told them they needed to sit in the back. King's father refused, stating "we'll either buy shoes sitting here or we won't buy any shoes at all", before taking King and leaving the store. He told King afterwards, "I don't care how long I have to live with this system, I will never accept it."

In 1936, King's father led hundreds of African-Americans in a civil rights march to the city hall in Atlanta, to protest voting rights discrimination. King later remarked that King Sr. was "a real father" to him.

King memorized and sang hymns, and stated verses from the Bible, by the time he was five years old. Over the next year, he began to go to church events with his mother and sing hymns while she played piano. His favorite hymn to sing was *"I Want to Be More and More Like Jesus"*; he moved attendees with his singing. King later became a member of the junior choir in his church. King enjoyed opera, and played the piano.

As he grew up, King garnered a large vocabulary from reading dictionaries and consistently used his expanding lexicon. He got into physical altercations with boys in his neighborhood, but oftentimes used his knowledge of words to stymie fights. King showed a lack of interest in

11

grammar and spelling, a trait which he carried throughout his life.

In 1939, King sang as a member of his church choir in slave costume, for the all-white audience at the Atlanta premiere of the film *Gone with the Wind*. In September 1940, at the age of 12, King was enrolled at the Atlanta University Laboratory School for the seventh grade. While there, King took violin and piano lessons, and showed keen interest in his history and English classes.

On May 18, 1941, when King had snuck away from studying at home to watch a parade, King was informed that something had happened to his maternal grandmother. Upon returning home, he found out that she had suffered a heart attack and died while being transported to a hospital. He took the death very hard, and believed that his deception of going to see the parade may have been responsible for God taking her. King jumped out of a second-story window at his home, but again survived an attempt to kill himself. His father instructed him in his bedroom that King shouldn't blame himself for her death, and that she had been called home to God as part of God's plan which could not be changed. King struggled with this, and could not fully believe that his parents knew where his grandmother had gone. Shortly thereafter, King's father decided to move the family to a two-story brick home on a hill that overlooked downtown Atlanta.

Adolescence

In his adolescent years, he initially felt resentment against whites due to the "racial humiliation" that he, his family, and his neighbors often had to endure in the segregated South.

In 1942, when King was 13 years old, he became the youngest assistant manager of a newspaper delivery station for the *Atlanta Journal*. That year, King skipped the ninth grade and was enrolled in Booker T. Washington High School, where he maintained a B-plus average. The high school was the only one in the city for African American students. It had been formed after local black leaders including King's grandfather (Williams), urged the city government of Atlanta to create it.

While King was brought up in a Baptist home, King grew skeptical of some of Christianity's claims as he entered adolescence. He began to question the literalist teachings preached at his father's church. At the age of 13, he denied the bodily resurrection of Jesus during Sunday school. King has stated, he found himself unable to identify with the emotional displays and gestures from congregants frequent at his church, and doubted if he would ever attain personal satisfaction from religion. He later stated of this point in his life, "doubts began to spring forth unrelentingly."

In high school, King became known for his public-speaking ability, with a voice which had grown into an orotund baritone. He proceeded to join the school's debate team. King continued to be most drawn to history and English, and choose English and sociology to be his main subjects while at the school. King maintained an abundant vocabulary. But, he relied on his sister, Christine, to help him with his spelling, while King assisted her with math. They studied in this manner routinely until Christine's graduation from high school. King also developed an interest in fashion, commonly adorning himself in well-polished patent leather shoes and tweed suits, which gained him the nickname "Tweed" or "Tweedie" among his friends. He further grew a liking for flirting with girls and dancing. His brother A. D. later remarked, "He kept flitting from chick to chick, and I decided I couldn't keep up with him. Especially since he was crazy about dances, and just about the best jitterbug in town."

On April 13, 1944, in his junior year, King gave his first public speech during an oratorical contest, sponsored by the Improved Benevolent and Protective Order of Elks of the World in Dublin, Georgia. In his speech he stated, "black America still wears chains. The finest negro is at the mercy of the meanest white man. Even winners of our highest honors face the class color bar." King was selected as the winner of the contest. On the ride home to Atlanta by bus, he and his teacher were ordered by the driver to stand so that white passengers could sit down. The driver of the bus called King a "black son-of-a-bitch". King initially refused but complied after his teacher told him that he would be breaking the law if he did not follow the directions of the driver. As all the seats were occupied, he and his teacher were forced to stand on the rest of the drive back to Atlanta. Later King wrote of the incident, saying "That night will never leave my memory. It was the angriest I have ever been in my life."

Morehouse College

"The function of education is to teach one to think intensively and to think critically. Intelligence plus character – that is the goal of true education." — Martin Luther King Jr

During King's junior year in high school, Morehouse College—an all-male historically black college which King's father and maternal grandfather had attended—began accepting high school juniors who passed the school's entrance examination. As World War II was underway many black college students had been enlisted in the war, decreasing the numbers of students at Morehouse College. So, the university aimed to increase their student numbers by allowing junior high school students to apply. In 1944, at the age of 15, King passed the entrance examination and was enrolled at the university for the school season that autumn.

In the summer before King started his freshman year at Morehouse, he boarded a train with his friend—Emmett "Weasel" Proctor—and a group of other Morehouse College students to work in Simsbury, Connecticut at the tobacco farm of Cullman Brothers Tobacco (a cigar business). This was King's first trip outside of the segregated south into the integrated north.

In a June 1944 letter to his father King wrote about the differences that struck him between the two parts of the country, "On our way here we saw some things I had never anticipated to see. After we passed Washington there was no discrimination at all. The white people here are very nice. We go to any place we want to and sit any where we want to." The students worked at the farm to be able to provide for their educational costs at Morehouse College, as the farm had partnered with the college to allot their salaries towards the university's tuition, housing, and other fees.

On weekdays King and the other students worked in the fields, picking tobacco from 7:00am till at least 5:00pm, enduring temperatures above 100°F, to earn roughly USD$4 per day. On Friday evenings, King and the other students visited downtown Simsbury to get milkshakes and watch movies, and on Saturdays they would travel to Hartford, Connecticut to see theatre performances, shop and eat in restaurants. While each Sunday they would go to Hartford to attend church services, at a church filled with white congregants. King wrote to his parents about the lack of segregation in Connecticut, relaying how he was amazed they could go to the "one of the finest restaurants in Hartford" and that "Negroes and whites go to the same church".

He played freshman football there. The summer before his last year at Morehouse, in 1947, the 18-year-old King chose to enter the ministry. Throughout his time in college, King studied under the mentorship of its president, Baptist minister Benjamin Mays, who he would later credit with being his "spiritual mentor." King had concluded that the church offered the most assuring way to answer "an inner urge to serve humanity." His "inner urge" had begun developing, and he made peace with the Baptist Church, as he believed he would be a "rational" minister with sermons that were "a respectful force for ideas, even social protest." King graduated from Morehouse with a Bachelor of Arts (BA) in sociology in 1948, aged nineteen.

Religious education, ministry, marriage and family

Crozer Theological Seminary

King enrolled in Crozer Theological Seminary in Upland, Pennsylvania. King's father fully supported his decision to continue his education and made arrangements for King to work with J. Pius Barbour, a family friend who pastored at Calvary Baptist Church in nearby Chester, Pennsylvania. King became known as one of the "Sons of Calvary", an honor he shared with William Augustus Jones Jr. and Samuel D. Proctor who both went on to become well-known preachers in the black church.

While attending Crozer, King was joined by Walter McCall, a former classmate at Morehouse. At Crozer, King was elected president of the student body. The African-American students of Crozer for the most part conducted their social activity on Edwards Street. King became fond of the street because a classmate had an aunt who prepared collard greens for them, which they both relished.

King once reproved another student for keeping beer in his room, saying they had shared responsibility as African Americans to bear "the burdens of the Negro race." For a time, he was interested in Walter Rauschenbusch's "social gospel." In his third year at Crozer, King became romantically involved with the white daughter of an immigrant German woman who worked as a cook in the cafeteria. The woman had been involved with a professor prior to her relationship with King. King planned to marry her, but friends advised against it, saying that an interracial marriage would provoke animosity from both blacks and whites, potentially damaging his chances of ever pastoring a church in the South. King tearfully told a friend that he could not endure his mother's pain over the marriage and broke the relationship off six months later. He continued to have lingering feelings toward the woman he left; one friend was quoted as saying, "He never recovered." King graduated with a B.Div. degree in 1951.

Boston University

In 1951, King began doctoral studies in systematic theology at Boston University. While pursuing doctoral studies, King worked as an assistant minister at Boston's historic Twelfth Baptist Church with Rev. William Hunter Hester. Hester was an old friend of King's father, and was an important influence on King. In Boston, King befriended a small cadre of local ministers his age, and sometimes guest pastored at their churches, including the Reverend Michael Haynes, associate pastor at Twelfth Baptist Church in Roxbury (and younger brother of jazz drummer Roy Haynes). The young men often held bull sessions in their various apartments, discussing theology, sermon style, and social issues.

King attended philosophy classes at Harvard University as an audit student in 1952 and 1953.

At the age of 25 in 1954, King was called as pastor of the Dexter Avenue Baptist Church in Montgomery, Alabama. King received his Ph.D. degree on June 5, 1955, with a dissertation (initially supervised by Edgar S. Brightman and, upon the latter's death, by Lotan Harold DeWolf) titled *A Comparison of the Conceptions of God in the Thinking of Paul Tillich and Henry Nelson Wieman.*

An academic inquiry in October 1991 concluded that portions of his doctoral dissertation had been plagiarized and he had acted improperly. However, "[d]espite its finding, the committee said that 'no thought should be given to the revocation of Dr. King's doctoral degree,' an action that the panel said would serve no purpose." The committee found that the dissertation still "makes an intelligent contribution to scholarship." A letter is now attached to the copy of King's dissertation held in the university library, noting that numerous passages were included without the appropriate quotations and citations

20

of sources. Significant debate exists on how to interpret King's plagiarism.

Marriage and family

"The group consisting of mother, father and child is the main educational agency of mankind." — Martin Luther King Jr

While studying at Boston University, he asked a friend from Atlanta named Mary Powell, who was a student at the New England Conservatory of Music, if she knew any nice Southern girls. Powell asked fellow student Coretta Scott if she was interested in meeting a Southern friend studying divinity. Scott was not interested in dating preachers, but eventually agreed to allow Martin to telephone her based on Powell's description and vouching. On their first phone call, King told Scott "I am like Napoleon at Waterloo before your charms," to which she replied "You haven't even met me." They went out for dates in his green Chevy. After the second date, King was certain Scott possessed the qualities he sought in a wife. She had been an activist at Antioch in undergrad, where Carol and Rod Serling were schoolmates.

King married Coretta Scott on June 18, 1953, on the lawn of her parents' house in her hometown of Heiberger, Alabama. They became the parents of four children: Yolanda King (1955–2007), Martin Luther King III (b. 1957), Dexter Scott King (b. 1961), and Bernice King (b. 1963). During their marriage, King limited Coretta's role in the civil rights movement, expecting her to be a housewife and mother.

21

In December 1959, after being based in Montgomery for five years, King announced his return to Atlanta at the request of the SCLC. In Atlanta, King served until his death as co-pastor with his father at the Ebenezer Baptist Church, and helped expand the Civil Rights Movement across the South.

Activism and organizational leadership

Montgomery bus boycott, 1955

In March 1955, Claudette Colvin—a fifteen-year-old black schoolgirl in Montgomery—refused to give up her bus seat to a white man in violation of Jim Crow laws, local laws in the Southern United States that enforced racial segregation. King was on the committee from the Birmingham African-American community that looked into the case; E. D. Nixon and Clifford Durr decided to wait for a better case to pursue because the incident involved a minor.

Nine months later on December 1, 1955, a similar incident occurred when Rosa Parks was arrested for refusing to give up her seat on a city bus. The two incidents led to the Montgomery bus boycott, which was urged and planned by Nixon and led by King. The boycott lasted for 385 days, and the situation became so tense that King's house was bombed. King was arrested during this campaign, which concluded with a United States District Court ruling in *Browder v. Gayle* that ended racial segregation on all Montgomery public buses. King's role in the bus boycott transformed him into a national figure and the best-known spokesman of the civil rights movement.

Southern Christian Leadership Conference

In 1957, King, Ralph Abernathy, Fred Shuttlesworth, Joseph Lowery, and other civil rights activists founded the Southern Christian Leadership Conference (SCLC). The group was created to harness the moral authority and organizing power of black churches to conduct nonviolent protests in the service of civil rights reform. The group was inspired by the crusades of evangelist Billy Graham, who befriended King, as well as the national organizing of the group In Friendship, founded by King allies Stanley Levison and Ella Baker. King led the SCLC until his death. The SCLC's 1957 Prayer Pilgrimage for Freedom was the first time King addressed a national audience.

Other civil rights leaders involved in the SCLC with King included: James Bevel, Allen Johnson, Curtis W. Harris, Walter E. Fauntroy, C. T. Vivian, Andrew Young, The Freedom Singers, Cleveland Robinson, Randolph Blackwell, Annie Bell Robinson Devine, Charles Kenzie Steele, Alfred Daniel Williams King, Benjamin Hooks, Aaron Henry and Bayard Rustin.

Fact: King's 'I Have a Dream' speech was not his first at the Lincoln Memorial: Six years before his iconic oration at the March on Washington, King was among the civil rights leaders who spoke in the shadow of the Great Emancipator during the Prayer Pilgrimage for Freedom on May 17, 1957.

The Gandhi Society

Harry Wachtel joined King's legal advisor Clarence B. Jones in defending four ministers of the SCLC in the libel case *New York Times Co. v. Sullivan*; the case was litigated in reference to the newspaper advertisement "Heed Their Rising Voices". Wachtel founded a tax-exempt fund to cover the expenses of the suit and to assist the nonviolent civil rights movement through a more effective means of fundraising. This organization was named the "Gandhi Society for Human Rights." King served as honorary president for the group. He was displeased with the pace that President Kennedy was using to address the issue of segregation.

In 1962, King and the Gandhi Society produced a document that called on the President to follow in the footsteps of Abraham Lincoln and issue an executive order to deliver a blow for civil rights as a kind of Second Emancipation Proclamation. Kennedy did not execute the order.

The FBI was under written directive from Attorney General Robert F. Kennedy when it began tapping King's telephone line in the fall of 1963. Kennedy was concerned that public allegations of communists in the SCLC would derail the administration's civil rights initiatives. He warned King to discontinue these associations and later felt compelled to issue the written directive that authorized the FBI to wiretap King and other SCLC leaders. FBI Director J. Edgar Hoover feared the civil rights movement and investigated the allegations of communist infiltration. When no evidence emerged to support this, the FBI used the incidental details caught on tape over the next five years in attempts to force King out of his leadership position in the COINTELPRO program.

King believed that organized, nonviolent protest against the system of southern segregation known as Jim Crow laws would lead to extensive media coverage of the struggle for black equality and voting rights. Journalistic accounts and televised footage of the daily deprivation and indignities suffered by Southern blacks, and of segregationist violence and harassment of civil rights workers and marchers, produced a wave of sympathetic public opinion that convinced the majority of Americans that the civil rights movement was the most important issue in American politics in the early 1960s.

King organized and led marches for blacks' right to vote, desegregation, labor rights, and other basic civil rights. Most of these rights were successfully enacted into the law of the United States with the passage of the Civil Rights Act of 1964 and the 1965 Voting Rights Act.

The SCLC put into practice the tactics of nonviolent protest with great success by strategically choosing the methods and places in which protests were carried out. There were often dramatic stand-offs with segregationist authorities, who sometimes turned violent.

"I am not interested in power for power's sake, but I'm interested in power that is moral, that is right and that is good." — Martin Luther King Jr

Survived knife attack, 1958

On September 20, 1958, King was signing copies of his book *Stride Toward Freedom* in Blumstein's department store in Harlem when he narrowly escaped death. Izola Curry—a mentally ill black woman who thought that King was conspiring against her with communists—stabbed him in the chest with a letter opener, which nearly impinged on the aorta. King received first aid by police officers Al Howard and Philip Romano. King underwent emergency surgery with three doctors: Aubre de Lambert Maynard, Emil Naclerio and John W. V. Cordice; he remained hospitalized for several weeks. Curry was later found mentally incompetent to stand trial.

Atlanta Sit-Ins, Prison Sentence, and the 1960 Elections

Georgia governor Ernest Vandiver expressed open hostility towards King's return to his hometown in late 1959. He claimed that "wherever M. L. King, Jr., has been there has followed in his wake a wave of crimes", and vowed to keep King under surveillance.

On May 4, 1960, several months after his return, King drove writer Lillian Smith to Emory University when police stopped them. King was cited for "driving without a license" because he had not yet been issued a Georgia license. King's Alabama license was still valid, and Georgia law did not mandate any time limit for issuing a local license. King paid a fine, but was apparently unaware that his lawyer agreed to a plea deal that also included a probationary sentence.

Meanwhile, the Atlanta Student Movement had been acting to desegregate businesses and public spaces in the city, organizing the Atlanta sit-ins from March 1960 onwards.

In August the movement asked King to participate in a mass October sit-in, timed to highlight how 1960's Presidential election campaign had ignored civil rights. The coordinated day of action took place on October 19. King participated in a sit-in at the restaurant inside Rich's, Atlanta's largest department store, and was among the many arrested that day. The authorities released everyone over the next few days, except for King. Invoking his probationary plea deal, judge J. Oscar Mitchell sentenced King on October 25 to four months of hard labor. Before dawn the next day, King was taken from his county jail cell and transported to a maximum-security state prison.

The arrest and harsh sentence drew nationwide attention. Many feared for King's safety, as he started a prison sentence with people convicted of violent crimes, many of them White and hostile to his activism. Both Presidential candidates were asked to weigh in, at a time when both parties were courting the support of Southern Whites and their political leadership including Governor Vandiver. Nixon, with whom King had a closer relationship prior to the sit-in, declined to make a statement despite a personal visit from Jackie Robinson requesting his intervention. Nixon's opponent John F. Kennedy called the governor (a Democrat) directly, enlisted his brother Robert to exert more pressure on state authorities, and also, at the personal request of Sargent Shriver, made a phone call to King's wife to express his sympathy and offer his help. The pressure from Kennedy and others proved effective, and King was released two days later. King's father decided to openly endorse Kennedy's candidacy for the November 8 election which he narrowly won.

After the October 19 sit-ins and following unrest, a 30-day truce was declared in Atlanta for desegregation negotiations. However, the negotiations failed and sit-ins and boycotts resumed in full swing for several months.

On March 7, 1961, a group of Black elders including King notified student leaders that a deal had been reached: the city's lunch counters would desegregate in fall 1961, in conjunction with the court-mandated desegregation of schools. Many students were disappointed at the compromise. In a large meeting March 10 at Warren Memorial Methodist Church, the audience was hostile and frustrated towards the elders and the compromise. King then gave an impassioned speech calling participants to resist the "cancerous disease of disunity," and helping to calm tensions.

Albany Movement, 1961

The Albany Movement was a desegregation coalition formed in Albany, Georgia, in November 1961. In December, King and the SCLC became involved. The movement mobilized thousands of citizens for a broad-front nonviolent attack on every aspect of segregation within the city and attracted nationwide attention.

When King first visited on December 15, 1961, he "had planned to stay a day or so and return home after giving counsel." The following day he was swept up in a mass arrest of peaceful demonstrators, and he declined bail until the city made concessions. According to King, "that agreement was dishonored and violated by the city" after he left town.

King returned in July 1962 and was given the option of forty-five days in jail or a $178 fine (equivalent to $1,500 in 2019); he chose jail. Three days into his sentence, Police Chief Laurie Pritchett discreetly arranged for King's fine to be paid and ordered his release. "We had witnessed persons being kicked off lunch counter stools ... ejected from churches ... and thrown into jail ... But for the first time, we witnessed being kicked out of jail." It was later acknowledged by the King Center that Billy Graham was the one who bailed King out of jail during this time.

After nearly a year of intense activism with few tangible results, the movement began to deteriorate. King requested a halt to all demonstrations and a "Day of Penance" to promote nonviolence and maintain the moral high ground. Divisions within the black community and the canny, low-key response by local government defeated efforts. Though the Albany effort proved a key lesson in tactics for King and the national civil rights movement, the national media was highly critical of King's role in the defeat, and the SCLC's lack of results contributed to a growing gulf between the organization and the more radical SNCC. After Albany, King sought to choose engagements for the SCLC in which he could control the circumstances, rather than entering into pre-existing situations.

Birmingham campaign, 1963

"Injustice anywhere is a threat to justice everywhere."
— Martin Luther King Jr

In April 1963, the SCLC began a campaign against racial segregation and economic injustice in Birmingham,

Alabama. The campaign used nonviolent but intentionally confrontational tactics, developed in part by Rev. Wyatt Tee Walker. Black people in Birmingham, organizing with the SCLC, occupied public spaces with marches and sit-ins, openly violating laws that they considered unjust.

King's intent was to provoke mass arrests and "create a situation so crisis-packed that it will inevitably open the door to negotiation." The campaign's early volunteers did not succeed in shutting down the city, or in drawing media attention to the police's actions. Over the concerns of an uncertain King, SCLC strategist James Bevel changed the course of the campaign by recruiting children and young adults to join in the demonstrations. *Newsweek* called this strategy a Children's Crusade.

During the protests, the Birmingham Police Department, led by Eugene "Bull" Connor, used high-pressure water jets and police dogs against protesters, including children. Footage of the police response was broadcast on national television news and dominated the nation's attention, shocking many white Americans and consolidating black Americans behind the movement. Not all of the demonstrators were peaceful, despite the avowed intentions of the SCLC. In some cases, bystanders attacked the police, who responded with force. King and the SCLC were criticized for putting children in harm's way. But the campaign was a success: Connor lost his job, the "Jim Crow" signs came down, and public places became more open to blacks. King's reputation improved immensely.

King was arrested and jailed early in the campaign—his 13th arrest out of 29. From his cell, he composed the now-famous "Letter from Birmingham Jail" that responds to calls on the movement to pursue legal channels for social change.

King argues that the crisis of racism is too urgent, and the current system too entrenched: "We know through painful experience that freedom is never voluntarily given by the oppressor; it must be demanded by the oppressed." He points out that the Boston Tea Party, a celebrated act of rebellion in the American colonies, was illegal civil disobedience, and that, conversely, "everything Adolf Hitler did in Germany was 'legal'." Walter Reuther, president of the United Auto Workers, arranged for $160,000 to bail out King and his fellow protestors.

March on Washington, 1963

King, representing the SCLC, was among the leaders of the "Big Six" civil rights organizations who were instrumental in the organization of the March on Washington for Jobs and Freedom, which took place on August 28, 1963. The other leaders and organizations comprising the Big Six were Roy Wilkins from the National Association for the Advancement of Colored People; Whitney Young, National Urban League; A. Philip Randolph, Brotherhood of Sleeping Car Porters; John Lewis, SNCC; and James L. Farmer Jr., of the Congress of Racial Equality.

Bayard Rustin's open homosexuality, support of socialism, and his former ties to the Communist Party USA caused many white and African-American leaders to demand King distance himself from Rustin, which

King agreed to do. However, he did collaborate in the 1963 March on Washington, for which Rustin was the primary logistical and strategic organizer. For King, this role was another which courted controversy, since he was one of the key figures who acceded to the wishes of United States President John F. Kennedy in changing the focus of the march.

Kennedy initially opposed the march outright, because he was concerned it would negatively impact the drive for passage of civil rights legislation. However, the organizers were firm that the march would proceed. With the march going forward, the Kennedys decided it was important to work to ensure its success. President Kennedy was concerned the turnout would be less than 100,000. Therefore, he enlisted the aid of additional church leaders and Walter Reuther, president of the United Automobile Workers, to help mobilize demonstrators for the cause.

The march originally was conceived as an event to dramatize the desperate condition of blacks in the southern U.S. and an opportunity to place organizers' concerns and grievances squarely before the seat of power in the nation's capital. Organizers intended to denounce the federal government for its failure to safeguard the civil rights and physical safety of civil rights workers and blacks. The group acquiesced to presidential pressure and influence, and the event ultimately took on a far less strident tone. As a result, some civil rights activists felt it presented an inaccurate, sanitized pageant of racial harmony; Malcolm X called it the "Farce on Washington", and the Nation of Islam forbade its members from attending the march.

The march made specific demands: an end to racial segregation in public schools; meaningful civil rights legislation, including a law prohibiting racial discrimination in employment; protection of civil rights workers from police brutality; a $2 minimum wage for all workers (equivalent to $17 in 2019); and self-government for Washington, D.C., then governed by congressional committee. Despite tensions, the march was a resounding success. More than a quarter of a million people of diverse ethnicities attended the event, sprawling from the steps of the Lincoln Memorial onto the National Mall and around the reflecting pool. At the time, it was the largest gathering of protesters in Washington, D.C.'s history.

King delivered a 17-minute speech, later known as "I Have a Dream". In the speech's most famous passage – in which he departed from his prepared text, possibly at the prompting of Mahalia Jackson, who shouted behind him, "Tell them about the dream!" – King said:

"I Have a Dream" came to be regarded as one of the finest speeches in the history of American oratory. The March, and especially King's speech, helped put civil rights at the top of the agenda of reformers in the United States and facilitated passage of the Civil Rights Act of 1964.

The original typewritten copy of the speech, including King's handwritten notes on it, was discovered in 1984 to be in the hands of George Raveling, the first African-American basketball coach of the University of Iowa. In 1963, Raveling, then 26 years old, was standing near the podium, and immediately after the oration, impulsively asked King if he could have his copy of the speech, and he got it.

The following is a fragment of King's famous speech:

"I have a dream that one day on the red hills of Georgia, the sons of former slaves and the sons of former slave owners will be able to sit down together at the table of brotherhood.

I have a dream that one day even the state of Mississippi, a state sweltering with the heat of injustice, sweltering with the heat of oppression will be transformed into an oasis of freedom and justice.

I have a dream that my four little children will one day live in a nation where they will not be judged by the color of their skin but by the content of their character. I have a dream today.

I have a dream that one day down in Alabama with its vicious racists, with its governor having his lips dripping with the words of interposition and nullification, one day right down in Alabama little black boys and black girls will be able to join hands with little white boys and white girls as sisters and brothers. I have a dream today.

I have a dream that one day every valley shall be exalted, every hill and mountain shall be made low, the rough places will be made plain, and the crooked places will be made straight, and the glory of the Lord shall be revealed, and all flesh shall see it together.

This is our hope. This is the faith that I go back to the South with. With this faith, we will be able to hew out of the mountain of despair a stone of hope. With this faith we will be able to transform the jangling discords of our nation into a beautiful symphony of brotherhood. With this faith we will be able to work together, to pray together, to struggle together, to go to jail together, to stand up for freedom together, knowing that we will be free one day."

St. Augustine, Florida, 1964

In March 1964, King and the SCLC joined forces with Robert Hayling's then-controversial movement in St. Augustine, Florida. Hayling's group had been affiliated with the NAACP but was forced out of the organization for advocating armed self-defense alongside nonviolent tactics. However, the pacifist SCLC accepted them. King and the SCLC worked to bring white Northern activists to St. Augustine, including a delegation of rabbis and the 72-year-old mother of the governor of Massachusetts, all of whom were arrested. During June, the movement marched nightly through the city, "often facing counter demonstrations by the Klan, and provoking violence that garnered national media attention." Hundreds of the marchers were arrested and jailed. During the course of this movement, the Civil Rights Act of 1964 was passed.

New York City, 1964

On February 6, 1964, King delivered the inaugural speech of a lecture series initiated at the New School called "The American Race Crisis." No audio record of his speech has been found, but in August 2013, almost 50 years later, the school discovered an audiotape with 15 minutes of a question-and-answer session that followed King's address. In these remarks, King referred to a conversation he had recently had with Jawaharlal Nehru in which he compared the sad condition of many African Americans to that of India's untouchables.

In his March 18,1964 interview by Robert Penn Warren, King compared his activism to his father's, citing his training in non-violence as a key difference. He also discusses the next phase of the civil rights movement and integration.

"We want all of our rights, we want them here, and we want them now." — Martin Luther King Jr

Selma voting rights movement and "Bloody Sunday", 1965

In December 1964, King and the SCLC joined forces with the Student Nonviolent Coordinating Committee (SNCC) in Selma, Alabama, where the SNCC had been working on voter registration for several months. A local judge issued an injunction that barred any gathering of three or more people affiliated with the SNCC, SCLC, DCVL, or any of 41 named civil rights leaders. This injunction temporarily halted civil rights activity until King defied it by speaking at Brown Chapel on January 2, 1965. During the 1965 march to Montgomery, Alabama, violence by state police and others against the peaceful marchers resulted in much publicity, which made racism in Alabama visible nationwide.

Acting on James Bevel's call for a march from Selma to Montgomery, Bevel and other SCLC members, in partial collaboration with SNCC, attempted to organize a march to the state's capital. The first attempt to march on March 7, 1965, at which King was not present, was aborted because of mob and police violence against the demonstrators. This day has become known as Bloody Sunday and was a major turning point in the effort to gain public support for the civil rights movement. It was the clearest demonstration up to that time of the dramatic potential of King and Bevel's nonviolence strategy.

On March 5, King met with officials in the Johnson Administration in order to request an injunction against any prosecution of the demonstrators. He did not attend the march due to church duties, but he later wrote, "If I had any idea that the state troopers would use the kind of brutality they did, I would have felt compelled to give up my church duties altogether to lead the line." Footage of police brutality against the protesters was broadcast extensively and aroused national public outrage.

King next attempted to organize a march for March 9. The SCLC petitioned for an injunction in federal court against the State of Alabama; this was denied and the judge issued an order blocking the march until after a hearing. Nonetheless, King led marchers on March 9 to the

Edmund Pettus Bridge in Selma, then held a short prayer session before turning the marchers around and asking them to disperse so as not to violate the court order. The unexpected ending of this second march aroused the surprise and anger of many within the local movement. Meanwhile, on March 11 King cried at the news of Johnson supporting a voting rights bill on television in Marie Foster's living room. The march finally went ahead fully on March 25, 1965. At the conclusion of the march on the steps of the state capitol, King delivered a speech that became known as "How Long, Not Long." In it, King stated that equal rights for African Americans could not be far away, "because the arc of the moral universe is long, but it bends toward justice" and "you shall reap what you sow".

Chicago open housing movement, 1966

In 1966, after several successes in the south, King, Bevel, and others in the civil rights organizations took the movement to the North, with Chicago as their first destination. King and Ralph Abernathy, both from the middle class, moved into a building at 1550 S. Hamlin Avenue, in the slums of North Lawndale on Chicago's West Side, as an educational experience and to demonstrate their support and empathy for the poor.

The SCLC formed a coalition with CCCO, Coordinating Council of Community Organizations, an organization founded by Albert Raby, and the combined organizations' efforts were fostered under the aegis of the Chicago Freedom Movement.During that spring, several white

41

couple/black couple tests of real estate offices uncovered racial steering: discriminatory processing of housing requests by couples who were exact matches in income, background, number of children, and other attributes. Several larger marches were planned and executed: in Bogan, Belmont Cragin, Jefferson Park, Evergreen Park (a suburb southwest of Chicago), Gage Park, Marquette Park, and others.

King later stated and Abernathy wrote that the movement received a worse reception in Chicago than in the South. Marches, especially the one through Marquette Park on August 5, 1966, were met by thrown bottles and screaming throngs. Rioting seemed very possible. King's beliefs militated against his staging a violent event, and he negotiated an agreement with Mayor Richard J. Daley to cancel a march in order to avoid the violence that he feared would result. King was hit by a brick during one march, but continued to lead marches in the face of personal danger.

When King and his allies returned to the South, they left Jesse Jackson, a seminary student who had previously joined the movement in the South, in charge of their organization. Jackson continued their struggle for civil rights by organizing the Operation Breadbasket movement that targeted chain stores that did not deal fairly with blacks.

A 1967 CIA document declassified in 2017 downplayed King's role in the "black militant situation" in Chicago, with a source stating that King "sought at least constructive, positive projects."

Opposition to the Vietnam War

King was long opposed to American involvement in the Vietnam War, but at first avoided the topic in public speeches in order to avoid the interference with civil rights goals that criticism of President Johnson's policies might have created. At the urging of SCLC's former Director of Direct Action and now the head of the Spring Mobilization Committee to End the War in Vietnam, James Bevel, and inspired by the outspokenness of Muhammad Ali, King eventually agreed to publicly oppose the war as opposition was growing among the American public.

During an April 4, 1967, appearance at the New York City Riverside Church—exactly one year before his death—

King delivered a speech titled "Beyond Vietnam: A Time to Break Silence." He spoke strongly against the U.S.'s role in the war, arguing that the U.S. was in Vietnam "to occupy it as an American colony" and calling the U.S. government "the greatest purveyor of violence in the world today." He connected the war with economic injustice, arguing that the country needed serious moral change:

A true revolution of values will soon look uneasily on the glaring contrast of poverty and wealth. With righteous indignation, it will look across the seas and see individual capitalists of the West investing huge sums of money in Asia, Africa and South America, only to take the profits out with no concern for the social betterment of the countries, and say: "This is not just."

King opposed the Vietnam War because it took money and resources that could have been spent on social welfare at home. The United States Congress was spending more and more on the military and less and less on anti-poverty programs at the same time. He summed up this aspect by saying, "A nation that continues year after year to spend more money on military defense than on programs of social uplift is approaching spiritual death." He stated that North Vietnam "did not begin to send in any large number of supplies or men until American forces had arrived in the tens of thousands", and accused the U.S. of having killed a million Vietnamese, "mostly children." King also criticized American opposition to North Vietnam's land reforms.

"Those who love peace must learn to organize as effectively as those who love war." — Martin Luther King Jr

King's opposition cost him significant support among white allies, including President Johnson, Billy Graham, union leaders and powerful publishers. "The press is being stacked against me", King said, complaining of what he described as a double standard that applauded his nonviolence at home, but deplored it when applied "toward little brown Vietnamese children." Life magazine called the speech "demagogic slander that sounded like a script for Radio Hanoi", and *The Washington Post* declared that King had "diminished his usefulness to his cause, his country, his people."

The "Beyond Vietnam" speech reflected King's evolving political advocacy in his later years, which paralleled the teachings of the progressive Highlander Research and Education Center, with which he was affiliated. King began to speak of the need for fundamental changes in the political and economic life of the nation, and more frequently expressed his opposition to the war and his desire to see a redistribution of resources to correct racial and economic injustice. He guarded his language in public to avoid being linked to communism by his enemies, but in private he sometimes spoke of his support for democratic socialism.

In a 1952 letter to Coretta Scott, he said: "I imagine you already know that I am much more socialistic in my economic theory than capitalistic ..." In one speech, he stated that "something is wrong with capitalism" and claimed, "There must be a better distribution of wealth, and maybe America must move toward a democratic socialism." King had read Marx while at Morehouse, but while he rejected "traditional capitalism", he rejected communism because of its "materialistic interpretation of history" that denied religion, its "ethical relativism", and its "political totalitarianism."

King stated in "Beyond Vietnam" that "true compassion is more than flinging a coin to a beggar ... it comes to see that an edifice which produces beggars needs restructuring." King quoted a United States official who said that from Vietnam to Latin America, the country was "on the wrong side of a world revolution." King condemned America's "alliance with the landed gentry of Latin America", and said that the U.S. should support "the shirtless and barefoot people" in the Third World rather than suppressing their attempts at revolution.

King's stance on Vietnam encouraged Allard K. Lowenstein, William Sloane Coffin and Norman Thomas, with the support of anti-war Democrats, to attempt to persuade King to run against President Johnson in the 1968 United States presidential election. King contemplated but ultimately decided against the proposal on the grounds that he felt uneasy with politics and considered himself better suited for his morally unambiguous role as an activist.

On April 15, 1967, King participated and spoke at an anti-war march from Manhattan's Central Park to the United Nations. The march was organized by the Spring Mobilization Committee to End the War in Vietnam and initiated by its chairman, James Bevel. At the U.N. King brought up issues of civil rights and the draft:

I have not urged a mechanical fusion of the civil rights and peace movements. There are people who have come to see the moral imperative of equality, but who cannot yet see the moral imperative of world brotherhood. I would like to see the fervor of the civil-rights movement imbued into the peace movement to instill it with greater strength. And I believe everyone has a duty to be in both the civil-rights and peace movements. But for those who presently choose but one, I would hope they will finally come to see the moral roots common to both.

Seeing an opportunity to unite civil rights activists and anti-war activists, Bevel convinced King to become even more active in the anti-war effort. Despite his growing public opposition towards the Vietnam War, King was not fond of the hippie culture which developed from the anti-war movement.

In his 1967 Massey Lecture, King stated:

The importance of the hippies is not in their unconventional behavior, but in the fact that hundreds of thousands of young people, in turning to a flight from reality, are expressing a profoundly discrediting view on the society they emerge from.

On January 13, 1968 (the day after President Johnson's State of the Union Address), King called for a large march on Washington against "one of history's most cruel and senseless wars."

We need to make clear in this political year, to congressmen on both sides of the aisle and to the president of the United States, that we will no longer tolerate, we will no longer vote for men who continue to see the killings of Vietnamese and Americans as the best way of advancing the goals of freedom and self-determination in Southeast Asia.

Correspondence with Thích Nhất Hạnh

Thích Nhất Hạnh was an influential Vietnamese Buddhist who taught at Princeton University and Columbia University. He had written a letter to Martin Luther King Jr. in 1965 entitled: "In Search of the Enemy of Man". It was during his 1966 stay in the US that Nhất Hạnh met with King and urged him to publicly denounce the Vietnam War.

In 1967, Dr. King gave a famous speech at the Riverside Church in New York City, his first to publicly question the U.S. involvement in Vietnam. Later that year, Dr. King nominated Nhất Hạnh for the 1967 Nobel Peace Prize. In his nomination Dr. King said, "I do not personally know of anyone more worthy of [this prize] than this gentle monk from Vietnam. His ideas for peace, if applied, would build a monument to ecumenism, to world brotherhood, to humanity".

Martin Luther King Jr "The Other America" *speech:*

On March 14, 1968, King gave a speech in Grosse Pointe High School to talk about the division that America was facing.

The following is a fragment of that speech:

"And so I want to use as a title for my lecture tonight, "The Other America." And I use this title because there are literally two Americas. Every city in our country has this kind of dualism, this schizophrenia, split at so many parts, and so every city ends up being two cities rather than one. There are two Americas.

One America is beautiful for situation. In this America, millions of people have the milk of prosperity and the honey of equality flowing before them. This America is the habitat of millions of people who have food and material necessities for their bodies, culture and education for their minds, freedom and human dignity for their spirits. In this America children grow up in the sunlight of opportunity.

But there is another America. This other America has a daily ugliness about it that transforms the buoyancy of hope into the fatigue of despair.

In this other America, thousands and thousands of people, men in particular walk the streets in search for jobs that do not exist. In this other America, millions of people are forced to live in vermin-filled, distressing housing conditions where they do not have the privilege of having wall-to-wall carpeting, but all too often, they end up with wall-to-wall rats and roaches. Almost forty percent of the Negro families of America live in sub-standard housing conditions.

In this other America, thousands of young people are deprived of an opportunity to get an adequate education. Every year thousands finish high school reading at a seventh, eighth and sometimes ninth grade level. Not

49

because they're dumb, not because they don't have the native intelligence, but because the schools are so inadequate, so over-crowded, so devoid of quality, so segregated if you will, that the best in these minds can never come out. Probably the most critical problem in the other America is the economic problem."

Poor People's Campaign, 1968

In 1968, King and the SCLC organized the "Poor People's Campaign" to address issues of economic justice. King traveled the country to assemble "a multiracial army of the poor" that would march on Washington to engage in nonviolent civil disobedience at the Capitol until Congress created an "economic bill of rights" for poor Americans.

The campaign was preceded by King's final book, *Where Do We Go from Here: Chaos or Community?* which laid out his view of how to address social issues and poverty. King quoted from Henry George and George's book, *Progress and Poverty*, particularly in support of a guaranteed basic income. The campaign culminated in a march on Washington, D.C., demanding economic aid to the poorest communities of the United States.

King and the SCLC called on the government to invest in rebuilding America's cities. He felt that Congress had shown "hostility to the poor" by spending "military funds with alacrity and generosity." He contrasted this with the situation faced by poor Americans, claiming that Congress had merely provided "poverty funds with miserliness." His vision was for change that was more revolutionary than mere reform: he cited systematic flaws of "racism, poverty, militarism and materialism", and argued that "reconstruction of society itself is the real issue to be faced."

The Poor People's Campaign was controversial even within the civil rights movement. Rustin resigned from the march, stating that the goals of the campaign were too broad, that its demands were unrealizable, and that he thought that these campaigns would accelerate the backlash and repression on the poor and the black.

Fact: From 1957 to 1968, King traveled over 6 million miles and spoke over 2,500 times

Assassination and aftermath

"If physical death is the price that I must pay to free my white brothers and sisters from a permanent death of the spirit, then nothing can be more redemptive." — Martin Luther King Jr

On March 29, 1968, King went to Memphis, Tennessee, in support of the black sanitary public works employees, who were represented by AFSCME Local 1733. The workers had been on strike since March 12 for higher wages and better treatment. In one incident, black street repairmen received pay for two hours when they were sent home because of bad weather, but white employees were paid for the full day.

On April 3, King addressed a rally and delivered his "I've Been to the Mountaintop" address at Mason Temple, the world headquarters of the Church of God in Christ. King's flight to Memphis had been delayed by a bomb threat against his plane. In the prophetic peroration of the last speech of his life, in reference to the bomb threat, King said the following:

And then I got to Memphis. And some began to say the threats, or talk about the threats that were out. What would happen to me from some of our sick white brothers?Well, I don't know what will happen now. We've got some difficult days ahead. But it doesn't matter with me now. Because I've been to the mountaintop. And I don't mind. Like anybody, I would like to live a long life. Longevity has its place. But I'm not concerned about that now. I just want to do God's will. And He's allowed me to go up to the mountain. And I've looked over. And I've seen the promised land. I may not get there with you. But I want you to know tonight, that we, as a people, will get to the promised land. So I'm happy, tonight. I'm not worried about anything. I'm not fearing any man. Mine eyes have seen the glory of the coming of the Lord.

King was booked in Room 306 at the Lorraine Motel (owned by Walter Bailey) in Memphis. Ralph Abernathy, who was present at the assassination, testified to the United States House Select Committee on Assassinations that King and his entourage stayed at Room 306 so often that it was known as the "King-Abernathy suite." According to Jesse Jackson, who was present, King's last words on the balcony before his assassination were spoken to musician Ben Branch, who was scheduled to perform that night at an event King was attending: "Ben, make sure you play 'Take My Hand, Precious Lord' in the meeting tonight. Play it real pretty."

King was fatally shot by James Earl Ray at 6:01 p.m., Thursday, April 4, 1968, as he stood on the motel's second-floor balcony. The bullet entered through his right cheek, smashing his jaw, then traveled down his spinal cord before lodging in his shoulder. Abernathy heard the shot from inside the motel room and ran to the balcony to find King on the floor. Jackson stated after the shooting that he cradled King's head as King lay on the balcony, but this account was disputed by other colleagues of King; Jackson later changed his statement to say that he had "reached out" for King.

After emergency chest surgery, King died at St. Joseph's Hospital at 7:05 p.m. According to biographer Taylor

Branch, King's autopsy revealed that though only 39 years old, he "had the heart of a 60 year old", which Branch attributed to the stress of 13 years in the civil rights movement. King is buried within Martin Luther King Jr. National Historical Park.

Aftermath

The assassination led to a nationwide wave of race riots in Washington, D.C., Chicago, Baltimore, Louisville, Kansas City, and dozens of other cities. Presidential candidate Robert F. Kennedy was on his way to Indianapolis for a campaign rally when he was informed of King's death. He gave a short, improvised speech to the gathering of supporters informing them of the tragedy and urging them to continue King's ideal of nonviolence. The following day, he delivered a prepared response in Cleveland. James Farmer Jr. and other civil rights leaders also called for non-violent action, while the more militant Stokely Carmichael called for a more forceful response. The city of Memphis quickly settled the strike on terms favorable to the sanitation workers.

The plan to set up a shantytown in Washington, D.C., was carried out soon after the April 4 assassination. Criticism of King's plan was subdued in the wake of his death, and the SCLC received an unprecedented wave of donations for the purpose of carrying it out. The campaign officially began in Memphis, on May 2, at the hotel where King was murdered. Thousands of demonstrators arrived on the National Mall and stayed for six weeks, establishing a camp they called "Resurrection City."

President Lyndon B. Johnson tried to quell the riots by making several telephone calls to civil rights leaders, mayors and governors across the United States and told politicians that they should warn the police against the unwarranted use of force. But his efforts didn't work out: "I'm not getting through," Johnson told his aides. "They're all holing up like generals in a dugout getting ready to watch a war." Johnson declared April 7 a national day of mourning for the civil rights leader. Vice President Hubert Humphrey attended King's funeral on behalf of the President, as there were fears that Johnson's presence might incite protests and perhaps violence.

At his widow's request, King's last sermon at Ebenezer Baptist Church was played at the funeral, a recording of his "Drum Major" sermon, given on February 4, 1968. In that sermon, King made a request that at his funeral no mention of his awards and honors be made, but that it be said that he tried to "feed the hungry", "clothe the naked", "be right on the [Vietnam] war question", and "love and serve humanity." His good friend Mahalia Jackson sang his favorite hymn, "Take My Hand, Precious Lord", at the funeral. The assassination helped to spur the enactment of the Civil Rights Act of 1968.

Two months after King's death, James Earl Ray—who was on the loose from a previous prison escape—was captured at London Heathrow Airport while trying to leave England on a false Canadian passport. He was using the alias Ramon George Sneyd on his way to white-ruled Rhodesia. Ray was quickly extradited to Tennessee and charged with King's murder. He confessed to the assassination on March 10, 1969, though he recanted this confession three days later. On the advice of his attorney

55

Percy Foreman, Ray pleaded guilty to avoid a trial conviction and thus the possibility of receiving the death penalty. He was sentenced to a 99-year prison term. Ray later claimed a man he met in Montreal, Quebec, with the alias "Raoul" was involved and that the assassination was the result of a conspiracy. He spent the remainder of his life attempting, unsuccessfully, to withdraw his guilty plea and secure the trial he never had. Ray died in 1998 at age 70.

Allegations of conspiracy

Ray's lawyers maintained he was a scapegoat similar to the way that John F. Kennedy's assassin Lee Harvey Oswald is seen by conspiracy theorists. Supporters of this assertion said that Ray's confession was given under pressure and that he had been threatened with the death penalty. They admitted that Ray was a thief and burglar, but claimed that he had no record of committing violent crimes with a weapon. However, prison records in different U.S. cities have shown that he was incarcerated on numerous occasions for charges of armed robbery.

In a 2008 interview with CNN, Jerry Ray, the younger brother of James Earl Ray, claimed that James was smart and was sometimes able to get away with armed robbery. Jerry Ray said that he had assisted his brother on one such robbery. "I never been with nobody as bold as he is," Jerry said. "He just walked in and put that gun on somebody, it was just like it's an everyday thing."

Those suspecting a conspiracy in the assassination point to the two successive ballistics tests which proved that a rifle similar to Ray's Remington Gamemaster had been the murder weapon. Those tests did not implicate Ray's specific rifle. Witnesses near King at the moment of his death said that the shot came from another location. They said that it came from behind thick shrubbery near the boarding house—which had been cut away in the days following the assassination—and not from the boarding house window. However, Ray's fingerprints were found on various objects (a rifle, a pair of binoculars, articles of clothing, a newspaper) that were left in the bathroom where it was determined the gunfire came from. An examination of the rifle containing Ray's fingerprints determined that at least one shot was fired from the firearm at the time of the assassination.

"No one really knows why they are alive until they know what they'd die for." — Martin Luther King Jr

In 1997, King's son Dexter Scott King met with Ray, and publicly supported Ray's efforts to obtain a new trial.

Two years later, King's widow Coretta Scott King and the couple's children won a wrongful death claim against Loyd Jowers and "other unknown co-conspirators." Jowers claimed to have received $100,000 to arrange King's assassination. The jury of six whites and six blacks found in favor of the King family, finding Jowers to be complicit in a conspiracy against King and that government agencies were party to the assassination. William F. Pepper represented the King family in the trial.

In 2000, the U.S. Department of Justice completed the investigation into Jowers' claims but did not find evidence to support allegations about conspiracy. The investigation report recommended no further investigation unless some new reliable facts are presented. A sister of Jowers admitted that he had fabricated the story so he could make $300,000 from selling the story, and she in turn corroborated his story in order to get some money to pay her income tax.

In 2002, *The New York Times* reported that a church minister, Rev. Ronald Denton Wilson, claimed his father,

Henry Clay Wilson—not James Earl Ray—assassinated King. He stated, "It wasn't a racist thing; he thought Martin Luther King was connected with communism, and he wanted to get him out of the way." Wilson provided no evidence to back up his claims.

King researchers David Garrow and Gerald Posner disagreed with William F. Pepper's claims that the government killed King. In 2003, Pepper published a book about the long investigation and trial, as well as his representation of James Earl Ray in his bid for a trial, laying out the evidence and criticizing other accounts. King's friend and colleague, James Bevel, also disputed the argument that Ray acted alone, stating, "There is no way a ten-cent white boy could develop a plan to kill a million-dollar black man."

In 2004, Jesse Jackson stated:

The fact is there were saboteurs to disrupt the march. And within our own organization, we found a very key person who was on the government payroll. So infiltration within, saboteurs from without and the press attacks. ... I will never believe that James Earl Ray had the motive, the money and the mobility to have done it himself. Our government was very involved in setting the stage for and I think the escape route for James Earl Ray.

Legacy

South Africa

King's legacy includes influences on the Black Consciousness Movement and civil rights movement in South Africa. King's work was cited by, and served as, an inspiration for South African leader Albert Lutuli, who fought for racial justice in his country and was later awarded the Nobel Prize.

United Kingdom

King influenced Irish politician and activist John Hume. Hume, the former leader of the Social Democratic and Labour Party, cited King's legacy as quintessential to the Northern Irish civil rights movement and the signing of the Good Friday Agreement, calling him "one of my great heroes of the century."

In the United Kingdom, The Northumbria and Newcastle Universities Martin Luther King Peace Committee exists to honor King's legacy, as represented by his final visit to the UK to receive an honorary degree from Newcastle University in 1967. The Peace Committee operates out of the chaplaincies of the city's two universities, Northumbria and Newcastle, both of which remain centres for the study of Martin Luther King and the US civil rights movement. Inspired by King's vision, it undertakes a range of activities across the UK as it seeks to "build cultures of peace."

In 2017, Newcastle University unveiled a bronze statue of King to celebrate the 50th anniversary of his honorary doctorate ceremony. The Students Union also voted to rename their bar Luthers.

United States

King has become a national icon in the history of American liberalism and American progressivism. His main legacy was to secure progress on civil rights in the U.S. Just days after King's assassination, Congress passed the Civil Rights Act of 1968. Title VIII of the Act, commonly known as the Fair Housing Act, prohibited discrimination in housing and housing-related transactions on the basis of race, religion, or national origin (later expanded to include sex, familial status, and disability). This legislation was seen as a tribute to King's struggle in his final years to combat residential discrimination in the U.S. The day following King's assassination, school teacher Jane Elliott conducted her first "Blue Eyes/Brown Eyes" exercise with her class of elementary school students in Riceville, Iowa. Her purpose was to help them understand King's death as it related to racism, something they little understood as they lived in a predominantly white community.

King's wife Coretta Scott King followed in her husband's footsteps and was active in matters of social justice and civil rights until her death in 2006. The same year that Martin Luther King was assassinated, she established the King Center in Atlanta, Georgia, dedicated to preserving his legacy and the work of championing nonviolent conflict resolution and tolerance worldwide. Their son, Dexter King, serves as the center's chairman. Daughter Yolanda King, who died in 2007, was a motivational speaker, author and founder of Higher Ground Productions, an organization specializing in diversity training.

Even within the King family, members disagree about his religious and political views about gay, lesbian, bisexual and transgender people. King's widow Coretta publicly said that she believed her husband would have supported gay rights. However, his youngest child, Bernice King, has said publicly that he would have been opposed to gay marriage.

On February 4, 1968, at the Ebenezer Baptist Church, in speaking about how he wished to be remembered after his death, King stated:

I'd like somebody to mention that day that Martin Luther King Jr. tried to give his life serving others. I'd like for somebody to say that day that Martin Luther King Jr. tried to love somebody.

I want you to say that day that I tried to be right on the war question. I want you to be able to say that day that I did try to feed the hungry. I want you to be able to say that day that I did try in my life to clothe those who were naked. I want you to say on that day that I did try in my life to visit those who were in prison. And I want you to say that I tried to love and serve humanity.

Yes, if you want to say that I was a drum major. Say that I was a drum major for justice. Say that I was a drum major for peace. I was a drum major for righteousness. And all of the other shallow things will not matter. I won't have any money to leave behind. I won't have the fine and luxurious things of life to leave behind. But I just want to leave a committed life behind.

King is remembered as a martyr by the Episcopal Church in the United States of America with an annual feast day on the anniversary of his death, April 4. The Evangelical Lutheran Church in America commemorates King liturgically on the anniversary of his birth, January 15.

On June 25, 2019, *The New York Times Magazine* listed Martin Luther King Jr. among hundreds of artists whose material was reportedly destroyed in the 2008 Universal Studios fire.

Martin Luther King Jr. Day

Beginning in 1971, cities such as St. Louis, Missouri, and states established annual holidays to honor King. At the White House Rose Garden on November 2, 1983, President Ronald Reagan signed a bill creating a federal holiday to honor King. Observed for the first time on January 20, 1986, it is called Martin Luther King Jr. Day.

Following President George H. W. Bush's 1992 proclamation, the holiday is observed on the third Monday of January each year, near the time of King's birthday. On January 17, 2000, for the first time, Martin Luther King Jr. Day was officially observed in all fifty U.S. states. Arizona (1992), New Hampshire (1999) and Utah (2000) were the last three states to recognize the holiday. Utah previously celebrated the holiday at the same time but under the name Human Rights Day.

"The ultimate measure of a man is not where he stands in moments of comfort and convenience, but where he stands at times of challenge and controversy." — Martin Luther King Jr

Ideas, influences, and political stances

Christianity

As a Christian minister, King's main influence was Jesus Christ and the Christian gospels, which he would almost always quote in his religious meetings, speeches at church, and in public discourses. King's faith was strongly based in Jesus' commandment of loving your neighbor as yourself, loving God above all, and loving your enemies, praying for them and blessing them. His nonviolent thought was also based in the injunction to *turn the other cheek* in the Sermon on the Mount, and Jesus' teaching of putting the sword back into its place (Matthew 26:52). In his famous Letter from Birmingham Jail, King urged action consistent with what he describes as Jesus' "extremist" love, and also quoted numerous other Christian pacifist authors, which was very usual for him. In another sermon, he stated:

Before I was a civil rights leader, I was a preacher of the Gospel. This was my first calling and it still remains my greatest commitment. You know, actually all that I do in civil rights I do because I consider it a part of my ministry. I have no other ambitions in life but to achieve excellence in the Christian ministry. I don't plan to run for any political office. I don't plan to do anything but remain a preacher. And what I'm doing in this struggle, along with many others, grows out of my feeling that the preacher must be concerned about the whole man.

King's private writings show that he rejected biblical literalism; he described the Bible as "mythological," doubted that Jesus was born of a virgin and did not believe that the story of Jonah and the whale was true.

"The Measure of A Man"

In 1959, King published a short book called *The Measure of A Man*, which contained his sermons "What is Man?" and "The Dimensions of a Complete Life." The sermons argued for man's need for God's love and criticized the racial injustices of Western civilization.

Nonviolence

Veteran African-American civil rights activist Bayard Rustin was King's first regular advisor on nonviolence. King was also advised by the white activists Harris Wofford and Glenn Smiley. Rustin and Smiley came from the Christian pacifist tradition, and Wofford and Rustin both studied Mahatma Gandhi's teachings. Rustin had applied nonviolence with the Journey of Reconciliation campaign in the 1940s, and Wofford had been promoting Gandhism to Southern blacks since the early 1950s.

King had initially known little about Gandhi and rarely used the term "nonviolence" during his early years of activism in the early 1950s. King initially believed in and practiced self-defense, even obtaining guns in his household as a means of defense against possible attackers. The pacifists guided King by showing him the alternative of nonviolent resistance, arguing that this would be a better means to accomplish his goals of civil rights than self-defense. King then vowed to no longer personally use arms.

In the aftermath of the boycott, King wrote *Stride Toward Freedom*, which included the chapter *Pilgrimage to Nonviolence*. King outlined his understanding of nonviolence, which seeks to win an opponent to friendship, rather than to humiliate or defeat him. The chapter draws from an address by Wofford, with Rustin and Stanley Levison also providing guidance and ghostwriting.

King was inspired by Gandhi and his success with nonviolent activism, and as a theology student, King described Gandhi as being one of the "individuals who greatly reveal the working of the Spirit of God". King had "for a long time ... wanted to take a trip to India." With assistance from Harris Wofford, the American Friends Service Committee, and other supporters, he was able to fund the journey in April 1959. The trip to India affected King, deepening his understanding of nonviolent resistance and his commitment to America's struggle for civil rights. In a radio address made during his final evening in India, King reflected, "Since being in India, I am more convinced than ever before that the method of nonviolent resistance is the most potent weapon available to oppressed people in their struggle for justice and human dignity."

King's admiration of Gandhi's nonviolence did not diminish in later years. He went so far as to hold up his example when receiving the Nobel Peace Prize in 1964, hailing the "successful precedent" of using nonviolence "in a magnificent way by Mohandas K. Gandhi to challenge the might of the British Empire ... He struggled only with the weapons of truth, soul force, non-injury and courage."

Another influence for King's nonviolent method was Henry David Thoreau's essay *On Civil Disobedience* and its theme of refusing to cooperate with an evil system. He also was greatly influenced by the works of Protestant theologians Reinhold Niebuhr and Paul Tillich, and said that Walter Rauschenbusch's *Christianity and the Social Crisis* left an "indelible imprint" on his thinking by giving him a theological grounding for his social concerns. King was moved by Rauschenbusch's vision of Christians spreading social unrest in "perpetual but friendly conflict" with the state, simultaneously critiquing it and calling it to act as an instrument of justice. However, he was apparently unaware of the American tradition of Christian pacifism exemplified by Adin Ballou and William Lloyd Garrison.

King frequently referred to Jesus' Sermon on the Mount as central for his work. King also sometimes used the concept of "agape" (brotherly Christian love). However, after 1960, he ceased employing it in his writings.

Even after renouncing his personal use of guns, King had a complex relationship with the phenomenon of self-defense in the movement. He publicly discouraged it as a widespread practice, but acknowledged that it was sometimes necessary. Throughout his career King was frequently protected by other civil rights activists who carried arms, such as Colonel Stone Johnson, Robert Hayling, and the Deacons for Defense and Justice.

Criticism within the movement

King was criticized by other black leaders during the course of his participation in the civil rights movement. This included opposition by more militant thinkers such as Nation of Islam member Malcolm X. Student Nonviolent Coordinating Committee founder Ella Baker regarded King as a charismatic media figure who lost touch with the grassroots of the movement as he became close to elite figures like Nelson Rockefeller. Stokely Carmichael, a protege of Baker's, became a black separatist and disagreed with King's plea for racial integration because he considered it an insult to a uniquely African-American culture.

Activism and involvement with Native Americans

"Our nation was born in genocide when it embraced the doctrine that the original American, the Indian, was an inferior race. Even before there were large numbers of Negroes on our shore, the scar of racial hatred had already disfigured colonial society." — Martin Luther King Jr

King was an avid supporter of Native American rights. Native Americans were also active supporters of King's civil rights movement which included the active participation of Native Americans. In fact, the Native American Rights Fund (NARF) was patterned after the NAACP's Legal Defense and Education Fund. The National Indian Youth Council (NIYC) was especially supportive in King's campaigns especially the Poor People's Campaign in 1968. In King's book *Why We Can't Wait* he writes:

From the sixteenth century forward, blood flowed in battles over racial supremacy. We are perhaps the only nation which tried as a matter of national policy to wipe out its indigenous population. Moreover, we elevated that tragic experience into a noble crusade. Indeed, even today we have not permitted ourselves to reject or to feel remorse for this shameful episode. Our literature, our films, our drama, our folklore all exalt it.

King assisted Native American people in south Alabama in the late 1950s. At that time the remaining Creek in Alabama were trying to completely desegregate schools in their area. The South had many egregious racial problems: In this case, light-complexioned Native children were allowed to ride school buses to previously all white schools, while dark-skinned Native children from the same band were barred from riding the same buses. Tribal leaders, upon hearing of King's desegregation campaign in Birmingham, Alabama, contacted him for assistance. He promptly responded and through his intervention the problem was quickly resolved.

In September 1959, King flew from Los Angeles, California, to Tucson, Arizona. After giving a speech at the University of Arizona on the ideals of using nonviolent methods in creating social change. He put into words his belief that one must not use force in this struggle "but match the violence of his opponents with his suffering." King then went to Southside Presbyterian, a predominantly Native American church, and was fascinated by their photos. On the spur of the moment Dr. King wanted to go to an Indian Reservation to meet the people so Reverend Casper Glenn took King to the Papago Indian Reservation.

At the reservation King met with all the tribal leaders, and others on the reservation then ate with them. King then visited another Presbyterian church near the reservation, and preached there attracting a Native American crowd. He later returned to Old Pueblo in March 1962 where he preached again to a Native American congregation, and then went on to give another speech at the University of Arizona. King would continue to attract the attention of Native Americans throughout the civil rights movement.

During the 1963 March on Washington there was a sizable Native American contingent, including many from South Dakota, and many from the Navajo nation. Native Americans were also active participants in the Poor People's Campaign in 1968.

King was a major inspiration along with the civil rights movement which inspired the Native American rights movement of the 1960s and many of its leaders. John Echohawk a member of the Pawnee tribe and the executive director and one of the founders of the Native American Rights Fund stated:

Inspired by Dr. King, who was advancing the civil rights agenda of equality under the laws of this country, we thought that we could also use the laws to advance our Indianship, to live as tribes in our territories governed by our own laws under the principles of tribal sovereignty that had been with us ever since 1831. We believed that we could fight for a policy of self-determination that was consistent with U.S. law and that we could govern our own affairs, define our own ways and continue to survive in this society.

Politics

As the leader of the SCLC, King maintained a policy of not publicly endorsing a U.S. political party or candidate: "I feel someone must remain in the position of nonalignment, so that he can look objectively at both parties and be the conscience of both—not the servant or master of either." In a 1958 interview, he expressed his view that neither party was perfect, saying, "I don't think the Republican party is a party full of the almighty God nor is the Democratic party. They both have weaknesses ... And I'm not inextricably bound to either party." King did praise Democratic Senator Paul Douglas of Illinois as being the "greatest of all senators" because of his fierce advocacy for civil rights causes over the years.

King critiqued both parties' performance on promoting racial equality:

Actually, the Negro has been betrayed by both the Republican and the Democratic party. The Democrats have betrayed him by capitulating to the whims and caprices of the Southern Dixiecrats. The Republicans have betrayed him by capitulating to the blatant hypocrisy of reactionary right-wing northern Republicans. And this coalition of southern Dixiecrats and right-wing reactionary northern Republicans defeats every bill and every move towards liberal legislation in the area of civil rights.

Although King never publicly supported a political party or candidate for president, in a letter to a civil rights supporter in October 1956 he said that he had not decided whether he would vote for Adlai Stevenson II or Dwight D. Eisenhower at the 1956 presidential election, but that "In the past, I always voted the Democratic ticket." In his autobiography, King says that in 1960 he privately voted for Democratic candidate John F. Kennedy: "I felt that Kennedy would make the best president. I never came out with an endorsement. My father did, but I never made one." King adds that he likely would have made an exception to his non-endorsement policy for a second Kennedy term, saying "Had President Kennedy lived, I would probably have endorsed him in 1964."

In 1964, King urged his supporters "and all people of goodwill" to vote against Republican Senator Barry Goldwater for president, saying that his election "would be a tragedy, and certainly suicidal almost, for the nation and the world."

King supported the ideals of democratic socialism, although he was reluctant to speak directly of this support due to the anti-communist sentiment being projected throughout the United States at the time, and the association of socialism with communism. King believed that capitalism could not adequately provide the necessities of many American people, particularly the African-American community.

Compensation

King stated that black Americans, as well as other disadvantaged Americans, should be compensated for historical wrongs. In an interview conducted for *Playboy* in 1965, he said that granting black Americans only equality could not realistically close the economic gap between them and whites. King said that he did not seek a full restitution of wages lost to slavery, which he believed impossible, but proposed a government compensatory program of $50 billion over ten years to all disadvantaged groups.

He posited that "the money spent would be more than amply justified by the benefits that would accrue to the nation through a spectacular decline in school dropouts, family breakups, crime rates, illegitimacy, swollen relief rolls, rioting and other social evils." He presented this idea as an application of the common law regarding settlement of unpaid labor, but clarified that he felt that the money should not be spent exclusively on blacks. He stated, "It should benefit the disadvantaged of *all* races."

Family planning

"Without love, there is no reason to know anyone, for love will, in the end, connect us to our neighbors, our children and our hearts." — Martin Luther King Jr

On being awarded the Planned Parenthood Federation of America's Margaret Sanger Award on May 5, 1966, King said:

Recently, the press has been filled with reports of sightings of flying saucers. While we need not give credence to these stories, they allow our imagination to speculate on how visitors from outer space would judge us. I am afraid they would be stupefied at our conduct. They would observe that for death planning we spend billions to create engines and strategies for war. They would also observe that we spend millions to prevent death by disease and other causes. Finally they would observe that we spend paltry sums for population planning, even though its spontaneous growth is an urgent threat to life on our planet. Our visitors from outer space could be forgiven if they reported home that our planet is inhabited by a race of insane men whose future is bleak and uncertain.

There is no human circumstance more tragic than the persisting existence of a harmful condition for which a remedy is readily available. Family planning, to relate population to world resources, is possible, practical and necessary. Unlike plagues of the dark ages or contemporary diseases we do not yet understand, the modern plague of overpopulation is soluble by means we have discovered and with resources we possess.

What is lacking is not sufficient knowledge of the solution but universal consciousness of the gravity of the problem and education of the billions who are its victims ...

Television

Actress Nichelle Nichols planned to leave the science-fiction television series *Star Trek* in 1967 after its first season, wanting to return to musical theater. She changed her mind after talking to King who was a fan of the show. King explained that her character signified a future of greater racial harmony and cooperation. King told Nichols, "You are our image of where we're going, you're 300 years from now, and that means that's where we are and it takes place now. Keep doing what you're doing, you are our inspiration." As Nichols recounted, "*Star Trek* was one of the only shows that [King] and his wife Coretta would allow their little children to watch. And I thanked him and I told him I was leaving the show. All the smile came off his face. And he said, 'Don't you understand for the first time we're seen as we should be seen. You don't have a black role. You have an equal role.'" For his part, the series' creator, Gene Roddenberry, was deeply moved upon learning of King's support.

Israel

King believed Israel has a right to exist, saying "Peace for Israel means security, and we must stand with all our might to protect her right to exist, its territorial integrity and the right to use whatever sea lanes it needs. Israel is one of the great outposts of democracy in the world, and a marvelous example of what can be done, how desert land can be transformed into an oasis of brotherhood and democracy. Peace for Israel means security, and that security must be a reality."

Homosexuality

A boy once asked King about how he should deal with his homosexuality. King replied:

Your problem is not at all an uncommon one. However, it does require careful attention. The type of feeling that you have toward boys is probably not an innate tendency, but something that has been culturally acquired. Your reasons for adopting this habit have now been consciously suppressed or unconsciously repressed. Therefore, it is necessary to deal with this problem by getting back to some of the experiences and circumstances that lead to the habit. In order to do this I would suggest that you see a good psychiatrist who can assist you in bringing to the forefront of conscience all of those experiences and circumstances that lead to the habit. You are already on the right road toward a solution, since you honestly recognize the problem and have a desire to solve it.

State surveillance and coercion

FBI surveillance and wiretapping

FBI director J. Edgar Hoover personally ordered surveillance of King, with the intent to undermine his power as a civil rights leader. The Church Committee, a 1975 investigation by the U.S. Congress, found that "From December 1963 until his death in 1968, Martin Luther King Jr. was the target of an intensive campaign by the Federal Bureau of Investigation to 'neutralize' him as an effective civil rights leader."

In the fall of 1963, the FBI received authorization from Attorney General Robert F. Kennedy to proceed with wiretapping of King's phone lines, purportedly due to his association with Stanley Levison. The Bureau informed President John F. Kennedy. He and his brother unsuccessfully tried to persuade King to dissociate himself from Levison, a New York lawyer who had been involved with Communist Party USA. Although Robert Kennedy only gave written approval for limited wiretapping of King's telephone lines "on a trial basis, for a month or so", Hoover extended the clearance so his men were "unshackled" to look for evidence in any areas of King's life they deemed worthy.

The Bureau placed wiretaps on the home and office phone lines of both Levison and King, and bugged King's rooms in hotels as he traveled across the country. In 1967, Hoover listed the SCLC as a black nationalist hate group, with the instructions: "No opportunity should be missed to exploit through counterintelligence techniques the organizational and personal conflicts of the leaderships of the groups ... to insure [sic] the targeted group is disrupted, ridiculed, or discredited."

NSA monitoring of King's communications

In a secret operation code-named "Minaret", the National Security Agency monitored the communications of leading Americans, including King, who were critical of the U.S. war in Vietnam. A review by the NSA itself concluded that Minaret was "disreputable if not outright illegal."

"Freedom is never voluntarily given by the oppressor; it must be demanded by the oppressed." — Martin Luther King Jr

Allegations of communism

For years, Hoover had been suspicious of potential influence of communists in social movements such as labor unions and civil rights. Hoover directed the FBI to track King in 1957, and the SCLC when it was established.

Due to the relationship between King and Stanley Levison, the FBI feared Levison was working as an "agent of influence" over King, in spite of its own reports in 1963 that Levison had left the Party and was no longer associated in business dealings with them. Another King lieutenant, Jack O'Dell, was also linked to the Communist

Party by sworn testimony before the House Un-American Activities Committee (HUAC).

Despite the extensive surveillance conducted, by 1976 the FBI had acknowledged that it had not obtained any evidence that King himself or the SCLC were actually involved with any communist organizations.

For his part, King adamantly denied having any connections to communism. In a 1965 *Playboy* interview, he stated that "there are as many Communists in this freedom movement as there are Eskimos in Florida." He argued that Hoover was "following the path of appeasement of political powers in the South" and that his concern for communist infiltration of the civil rights movement was meant to "aid and abet the salacious claims of southern racists and the extreme right-wing elements." Hoover did not believe King's pledge of innocence and replied by saying that King was "the most notorious liar in the country."

After King gave his "I Have A Dream" speech during the March on Washington on August 28, 1963, the FBI described King as "the most dangerous and effective Negro leader in the country." It alleged that he was "knowingly, willingly and regularly cooperating with and taking guidance from communists."

The attempts to prove that King was a communist was related to the feeling of many segregationists that blacks in the South were content with the status quo, but had been stirred up by "communists" and "outside agitators." As context, the civil rights movement in 1950s and '60s arose from activism within the black community dating back to before World War I. King said that "the Negro revolution is a genuine revolution, born from the same womb that produces all massive social upheavals—the womb of intolerable conditions and unendurable situations."

CIA surveillance

CIA files declassified in 2017 revealed that the agency was investigating possible links between King and Communism after a Washington Post article dated November 4, 1964 claimed he was invited to the Soviet Union and that Ralph Abernathy, as spokesman for King, refused to comment on the source of the invitation. Mail belonging to King and other civil rights activists was intercepted by the CIA program HTLINGUAL.

Allegations of adultery and involvement in a sexual assault

The FBI having concluded that King was dangerous due to communist infiltration, attempts to discredit King began through revelations regarding his private life. FBI surveillance of King, some of it since made public, attempted to demonstrate that he also had numerous extramarital affairs. Lyndon B. Johnson once said that King was a "hypocritical preacher".

In his 1989 autobiography *And the Walls Came Tumbling Down*, Ralph Abernathy stated that King had a "weakness for women", although they "all understood and believed in the biblical prohibition against sex outside of marriage. It was just that he had a particularly difficult time with that temptation."

In a later interview, Abernathy said that he only wrote the term "womanizing", that he did not specifically say King had extramarital sex and that the infidelities King had were emotional rather than sexual.

Abernathy criticized the media for sensationalizing the statements he wrote about King's affairs, such as the allegation that he admitted in his book that King had a sexual affair the night before he was assassinated. In his original wording, Abernathy had stated that he saw King coming out of his room with a woman when he awoke the next morning and later said that "he may have been in there discussing and debating and trying to get her to go along with the movement, I don't know...the Sanitation Worker's Strike."

In his 1986 book *Bearing the Cross*, David Garrow wrote about a number of extramarital affairs, including one woman King saw almost daily. According to Garrow, "that relationship ... increasingly became the emotional centerpiece of King's life, but it did not eliminate the incidental couplings ... of King's travels." He alleged that King explained his extramarital affairs as "a form of anxiety reduction." Garrow asserted that King's supposed promiscuity caused him "painful and at times overwhelming guilt." King's wife Coretta appeared to have accepted his affairs with equanimity, saying once that "all that other business just doesn't have a place in the very high level relationship we enjoyed."

Shortly after *Bearing the Cross* was released, civil rights author Howell Raines gave the book a positive review but opined that Garrow's allegations about King's sex life were "sensational" and stated that Garrow was "amassing facts rather than analyzing them."

The FBI distributed reports regarding such affairs to the executive branch, friendly reporters, potential coalition partners and funding sources of the SCLC, and King's family. The bureau also sent anonymous letters to King threatening to reveal information if he did not cease his civil rights work. The FBI–King suicide letter sent to King just before he received the Nobel Peace Prize read, in part:

The American public, the church organizations that have been helping—Protestants, Catholics and Jews will know you for what you are—an evil beast. So will others who have backed you. You are done. King, there is only one thing left for you to do. You know what it is. You have just 34 days in which to do (this exact number has been selected for a specific reason, it has definite practical significant [*sic*]). You are done. There is but one way out for you. You better take it before your filthy fraudulent self is bared to the nation.

The letter was accompanied by a tape recording—excerpted from FBI wiretaps—of several of King's extramarital liaisons. King interpreted this package as an attempt to drive him to suicide, although William Sullivan, head of the Domestic Intelligence Division at the time, argued that it may have only been intended to "convince Dr. King to resign from the SCLC." King refused to give in to the FBI's threats.

In 1977, Judge John Lewis Smith Jr. ordered all known copies of the recorded audiotapes and written transcripts resulting from the FBI's electronic surveillance of King between 1963 and 1968 to be held in the National Archives and sealed from public access until 2027.

In May 2019, FBI files emerged indicating that King "looked on, laughed and offered advice" as one of his friends raped a woman. His biographer, David Garrow, wrote that "the suggestion... that he either actively tolerated or personally employed violence against any woman, even while drunk, poses so fundamental a challenge to his historical stature as to require the most complete and extensive historical review possible". These allegations sparked a heated debate among historians.

Clayborne Carson, Martin Luther King biographer and overseer of the Dr. King records at Stanford University states that he came to the opposite conclusion of Garrow saying "None of this is new. Garrow is talking about a recently added summary of a transcript of a 1964 recording from the Willard Hotel that others, including Mrs. King, have said they did not hear Martin's voice on it. The added summary was four layers removed from the actual recording. This supposedly new information comes from an anonymous source in a single paragraph in an FBI report. You have to ask how could anyone conclude King looked at a rape from an audio recording in a room where he was not present." Carson bases his position of Coretta Scott King's memoirs where she states "I set up our reel-to-reel recorder and listened. I have read scores of reports talking about the scurrilous activities of my husband but once again, there was nothing at all incriminating on the tape. It was a social event with people laughing and telling dirty jokes. But I did not hear Martin's voice on it, and there was nothing about sex or anything else resembling the lies J. Edgar and the FBI were spreading." The tapes that could confirm or refute the allegation are scheduled to be declassified in 2027.

Police observation during the assassination

"Our lives begin to end the day we become silent about things that matter." — Martin Luther King Jr

A fire station was located across from the Lorraine Motel, next to the boarding house in which James Earl Ray was staying. Police officers were stationed in the fire station to keep King under surveillance. Agents were watching King at the time he was shot. Immediately following the shooting, officers rushed out of the station to the motel.

Marrell McCollough, an undercover police officer, was the first person to administer first aid to King. The antagonism between King and the FBI, the lack of an all points bulletin to find the killer, and the police presence nearby led to speculation that the FBI was involved in the assassination.

Awards and recognition

King was awarded at least fifty honorary degrees from colleges and universities. On October 14, 1964, King became the (at the time) youngest winner of the Nobel Peace Prize, which was awarded to him for leading nonviolent resistance to racial prejudice in the U.S. In 1965, he was awarded the American Liberties Medallion by the American Jewish Committee for his "exceptional advancement of the principles of human liberty." In his acceptance remarks, King said, "Freedom is one thing. You have it all or you are not free."

In 1957, he was awarded the Spingarn Medal from the NAACP. Two years later, he won the Anisfield-Wolf Book Award for his book *Stride Toward Freedom: The Montgomery Story*.

In 1966, the Planned Parenthood Federation of America awarded King the Margaret Sanger Award for "his courageous resistance to bigotry and his lifelong dedication to the advancement of social justice and human dignity." Also in 1966, King was elected as a fellow of the American Academy of Arts and Sciences. In November 1967 he made a 24-hour trip to the United Kingdom to receive an honorary degree from Newcastle University, being the first African-American to be so honoured by Newcastle. In a moving impromptu acceptance speech, he said:

There are three urgent and indeed great problems that we face not only in the United States of America but all over the world today. That is the problem of racism, the problem of poverty and the problem of war.

In addition to being nominated for three Grammy Awards, the civil rights leader posthumously won for Best Spoken Word Recording in 1971 for "Why I Oppose The War In Vietnam".

In 1977, the Presidential Medal of Freedom was posthumously awarded to King by President Jimmy Carter. The citation read:

Martin Luther King Jr. was the conscience of his generation. He gazed upon the great wall of segregation and saw that the power of love could bring it down. From the pain and exhaustion of his fight to fulfill the promises of our founding fathers for our humblest citizens, he wrung his eloquent statement of his dream for America. He made our nation stronger because he made it better. His dream sustains us yet.

King and his wife were also awarded the Congressional Gold Medal in 2004.

King was second in Gallup's List of Most Widely Admired People of the 20th Century. In 1963, he was named *Time* Person of the Year, and in 2000, he was voted sixth in an online "Person of the Century" poll by the same magazine. King placed third in the Greatest American contest conducted by the Discovery Channel and AOL.

Five-dollar bill

On April 20, 2016, Treasury Secretary Jacob Lew announced that the $5, $10, and $20 bills would all undergo redesign prior to 2020. Lew said that while Lincoln would remain on the front of the $5 bill, the reverse would be redesigned to depict various historical events that had occurred at the Lincoln Memorial. Among the planned designs are images from King's "I Have a Dream" speech and the 1939 concert by opera singer Marian Anderson.